A MAZE ADVENTURE

Storming a Castle

For my son Graham—G.W.

The publisher and packager wish to thank Christopher Gravett, Senior Curator in the Royal Armouries, Tower of London, and Barbara Grant, medieval scholar, for their expert assistance in reviewing the text and art in *Storming a Castle*.

The art was created by Graham White on computer with watercolor software.

Published by the National Geographic Society.

Prepared for the National Geographic Society by Firecrest Books Ltd.

Book design by Phil Jacobs

The text of the book is set in Galliard.

Library of Congress Cataloging-in-Publication Data:
Available upon request

ISBN 0-7922-6940-3

One of the world's largest nonprofit scientific and educational organizations, the National Geographic Society was founded in 1888 "for the increase and diffusion of geographic knowledge." Fulfilling this mission, the Society educates and inspires millions every day through its magazines, books, television programs, videos, maps and atlases, research grants, the National Geographic Bee, teacher workshops, and innovative classroom materials. The Society is supported through membership dues, charitable gifts, and income from the sale of its educational products. This support is vital to National Geographic's mission to increase global understanding and promote conservation of our planet through exploration, research, and education.

For more information, please call
1-800-NGS-LINE (647-5463) or write to the following address:
National Geographic Society
1145 17th Street N.W.
Washington, D.C. 20036-4688
U.S.A.

Visit the Society's Web site: www.nationalgeographic.com

Printed in Belgium

A MAZE ADVENTURE

Storming a Castle

Graham White

NATIONAL GEOGRAPHIC

Washington, D.C.

Contents

While taking every care to check the facts presented in this book and the validity of the drawings, the publishers have allowed a certain amount of "artistic license" to enable the artist to create the mazes and tell a story. This has involved, for example, the inclusion of staircases, ladders, openings, etc., to provide the routes and spaces needed for the mazes. In addition, the dungeon and torture aspects of the story were the exception rather than the rule to life inside a medieval castle and have been included to enhance the adventure. The coded puzzle is entirely fictional.

To complete the mazes, follow the clearly defined paths. You may go up and down stairs and ladders, behind pillars, etc., but no hopping over low walls or other obstructions that might look easy to climb over.

Welcome to the Middle Ages!

This is a time of great castles, knights in shining armor, jousting, and jesters. My name is Richard, and I'm 12 years old. I'm just taking a quick break from cleaning my father's sword.

I'm very excited. My father, a knight serving our king, is part of a great army, and we have traveled far across this land to a large castle, which is now only a short distance away. The lord and his family, who live in the castle, are very cruel. Not content with what he has, the lord has sent out his armies to take more villages and land for himself. As a result, many good and hard-working people have been killed trying to defend themselves and protect their possessions. So we are here to stop his cruelty and greed once and for all. Sent by our king, we have come to lay siege, hoping to take the castle and rid the land of this evil family so that everyone can live peacefully again.

In a day or two, we shall set up camp outside the castle walls and begin the hard work of preparing for battle. We have many machines to build that will help us get into the castle. My father has told me about them and even made me models from wood that really work. I can't wait to see the real thing!

I've waited a long time, too, to see a real castle. But my father says that, when we get closer, I should stay at the camp and help make arrows, prepare food, and tend to the injured. He says that the bowmen in the castle have trained all their lives to shoot very accurately, and if I wander too close they might part my hair with one of their arrows!

I'm hoping, though, that when the siege begins everybody will be far too busy to notice me. I'll be able to sneak into the castle to explore, and perhaps cause some mischief to our enemy.

Would you like to come with me? You would? Good! My father has taught me lots about how castles are built, so I'll explain things as we go.

We'll start by having a look at a plan of the castle on the next page.

I asked my father about the siege, and he gave me this plan of the castle to study. Just look at it! This place is huge! The cruel lord and his family live in the large building at the rear—it's called the "keep." See if you can find your way to it on the plan—it may help us later. Once our army has taken the keep, the castle will be ours!

This castle, like many others, has a deep area of water around it called a "moat." This makes it more difficult for us to attack and is our first obstacle as we approach. My father told me the extra gatehouse, called a "barbican," has been built in the moat and will make it even more difficult to get in through the main entrance. This is because we have to run across a stone "island" in the moat where we are vulnerable to the shower of arrows from the main gateway, towers, and walls.

The main defenses of the castle are the huge thick outer walls and the towers that support them. When we attack, there may be dozens of bowmen raining arrows down onto us from the tops of the walls and through narrow slots in the walls. On the plan you can see other, similar walls inside the castle that we will have to get past, too, before we reach the keep. This is not going to be easy!

Our army will try to cause fires in the castle by using flaming arrows and missiles. But many of the castle's roofs are made of tile, slate, or even lead sheets to prevent them from burning. Other wooden parts of the castle are protected by animal skins, which are fixed to them and kept wet throughout the battle. We use this method ourselves on our wooden machines, which would easily burn otherwise.

It will take a long time to prepare for the attack, but we have time on our side. The longer we are here, the more their supplies will dwindle. And if they run out altogether, who knows, we may even take the castle without a battle at all!

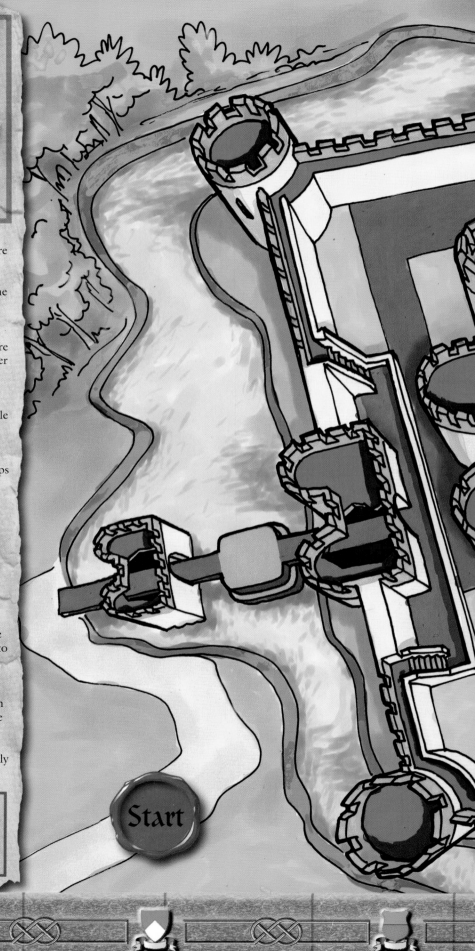

Start

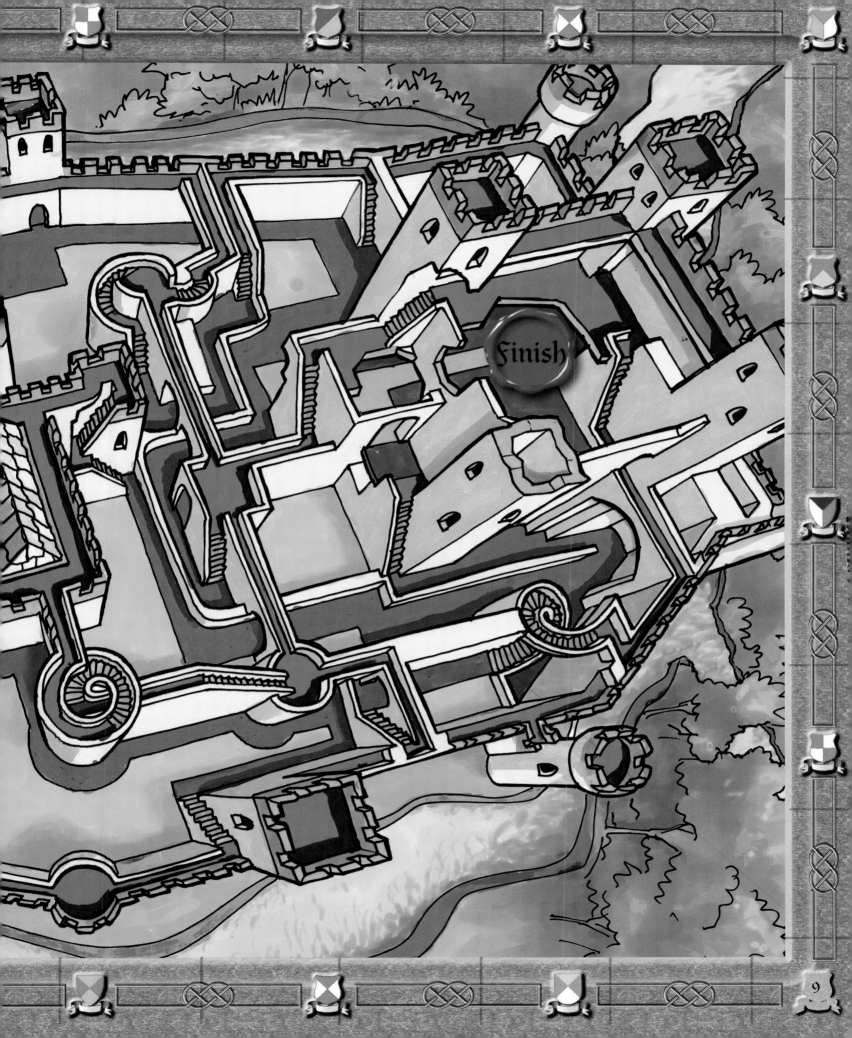

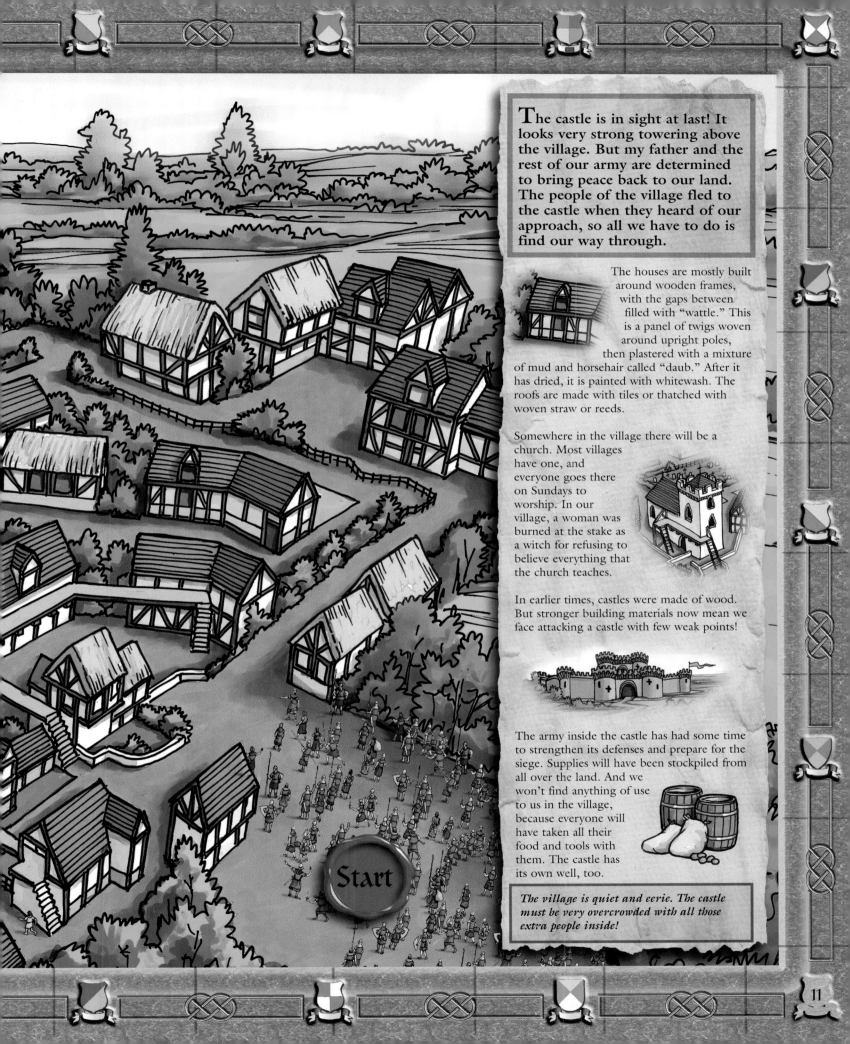

The castle is in sight at last! It looks very strong towering above the village. But my father and the rest of our army are determined to bring peace back to our land. The people of the village fled to the castle when they heard of our approach, so all we have to do is find our way through.

The houses are mostly built around wooden frames, with the gaps between filled with "wattle." This is a panel of twigs woven around upright poles, then plastered with a mixture of mud and horsehair called "daub." After it has dried, it is painted with whitewash. The roofs are made with tiles or thatched with woven straw or reeds.

Somewhere in the village there will be a church. Most villages have one, and everyone goes there on Sundays to worship. In our village, a woman was burned at the stake as a witch for refusing to believe everything that the church teaches.

In earlier times, castles were made of wood. But stronger building materials now mean we face attacking a castle with few weak points!

The army inside the castle has had some time to strengthen its defenses and prepare for the siege. Supplies will have been stockpiled from all over the land. And we won't find anything of use to us in the village, because everyone will have taken all their food and tools with them. The castle has its own well, too.

The village is quiet and eerie. The castle must be very overcrowded with all those extra people inside!

Start

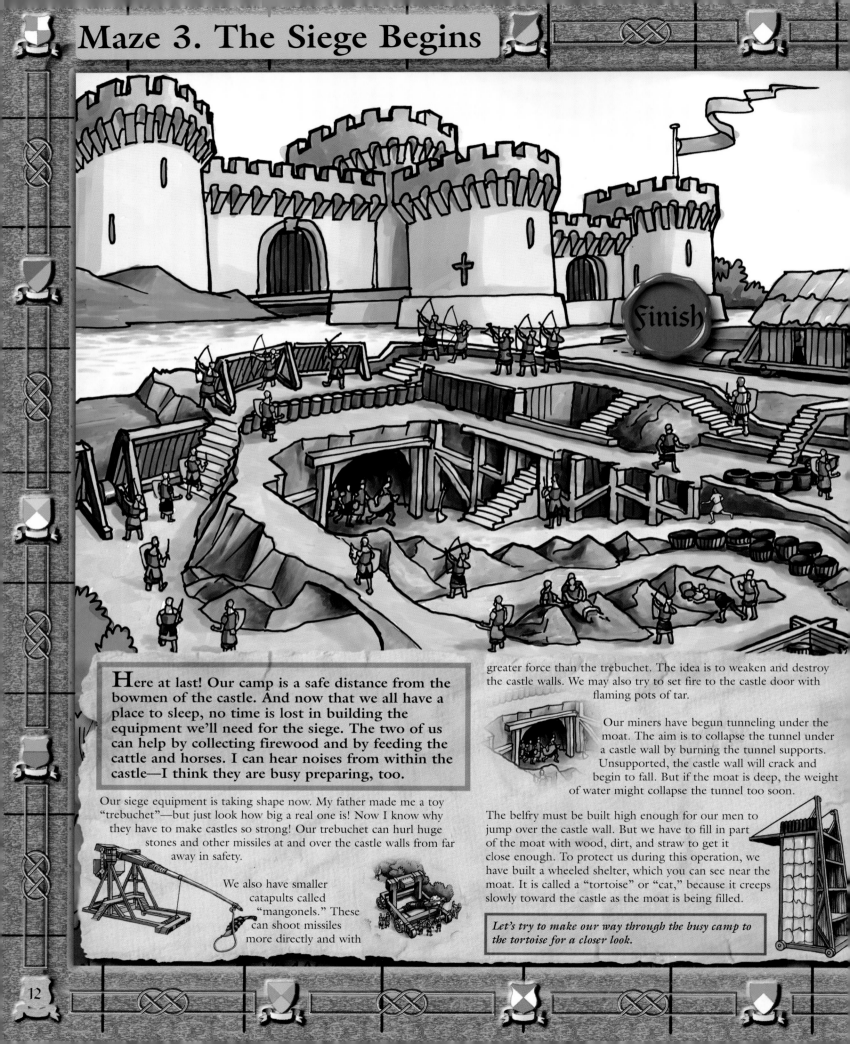

Finish

Here at last! Our camp is a safe distance from the bowmen of the castle. And now that we all have a place to sleep, no time is lost in building the equipment we'll need for the siege. The two of us can help by collecting firewood and by feeding the cattle and horses. I can hear noises from within the castle—I think they are busy preparing, too.

Our siege equipment is taking shape now. My father made me a toy "trebuchet"—but just look how big a real one is! Now I know why they have to make castles so strong! Our trebuchet can hurl huge stones and other missiles at and over the castle walls from far away in safety.

We also have smaller catapults called "mangonels." These can shoot missiles more directly and with greater force than the trebuchet. The idea is to weaken and destroy the castle walls. We may also try to set fire to the castle door with flaming pots of tar.

Our miners have begun tunneling under the moat. The aim is to collapse the tunnel under a castle wall by burning the tunnel supports. Unsupported, the castle wall will crack and begin to fall. But if the moat is deep, the weight of water might collapse the tunnel too soon.

The belfry must be built high enough for our men to jump over the castle wall. But we have to fill in part of the moat with wood, dirt, and straw to get it close enough. To protect us during this operation, we have built a wheeled shelter, which you can see near the moat. It is called a "tortoise" or "cat," because it creeps slowly toward the castle as the moat is being filled.

Let's try to make our way through the busy camp to the tortoise for a closer look.

Start

The attack has begun! Our brave knights and soldiers are fighting their way in, and some have reached the main gatehouse. But there is still a long way to go, and the enemy has many defenses. I just saw my father on the other side of the moat, but now he's disappeared. I must see if he's OK! Come on, let's go!

Look out! I've never seen so many arrows—and all heading this way! Archers shoot and reload in a blur of speed. It's a good thing we found shields to protect us, but I'm not sure this was such a good idea after all. Watch out! The soldiers on top of the castle are spilling burning tar and pouring quicklime that could burn our skin. Hurry! We need some shelter!

At last we've reached the gatehouse. But we must be careful—father warned me about "murder holes" in the ceiling. Archers fire through these when our soldiers become trapped between the huge gates. Our men have no chance and are just picked off one by one. So let's go this way...I bet that's where father went!

The belfry has reached the castle wall, and our men are able to jump over into the castle. We also have long ladders with hooks on top to secure them, but so far our men have not been so successful. The enemy has long sticks to push them away from the castle walls. It's an awfully long way down for our men to fall!

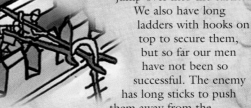

The small door in the castle wall is called a "sally port." Soldiers use it to sneak out in secret. They may launch a sudden attack, or "sally," from the sally port, charging out in force to attack our camp or destroy our machines.

Quickly, we must find our way through the gatehouse to the courtyard inside before we are discovered. I hope father is there!

Start

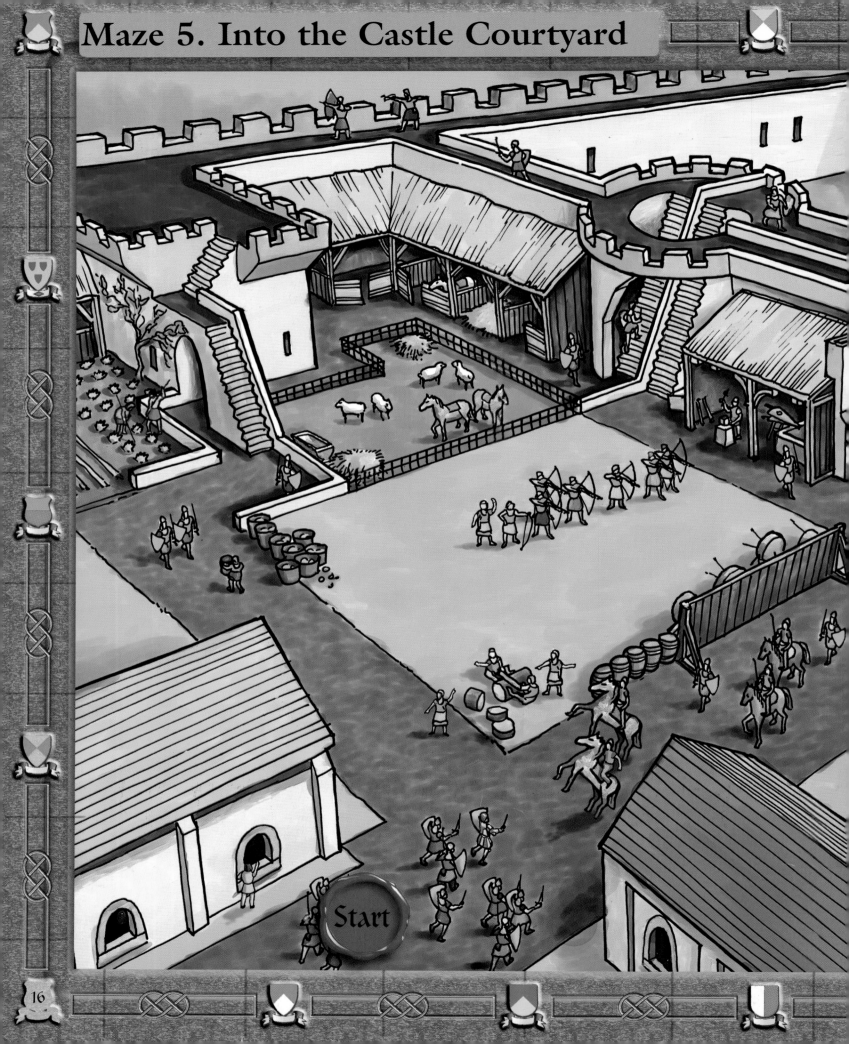

Start

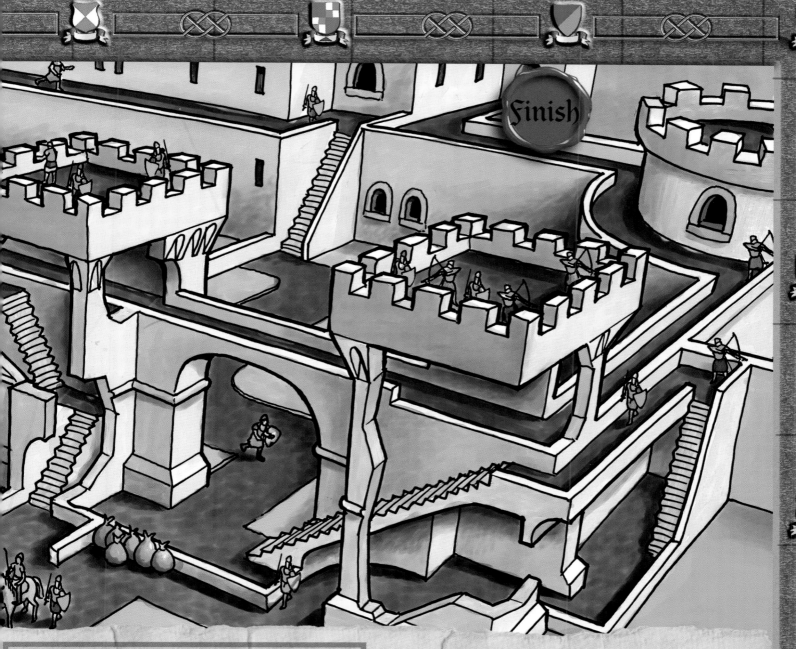

Finish

Inside the courtyard at last! My father is one of the first to break through, so he'll have plenty of fighting to do. But he is strong and brave. There are lots of storage barns for us to hide in, so we can keep out of the way. But look, what's this? A huge hoard of arrows! No time to waste—let's begin breaking them!

Looks like they didn't expect us just yet! The younger men of the castle are still practicing their archery skills. Learning to fight and to use longbows and crossbows is taught from a very early age.

The castle is a busy place in peacetime, too, with a bakehouse, brewhouse, workshops, stabling, and storage for food, firewood, and weapons. Many trades and skills are practiced within the walls—by stonemasons, carpenters,

and others. A blacksmith makes horseshoes and nails, while armorers make weapons.

Many animals are kept in and around the castle. Sheep are bred for meat and wool. Pigs are cheap to feed and easily kept, but the smell is terrible! Pigeons and geese make a tasty dish, and pigeons are also used to send messages. We have brought a basket of pigeons with us to keep our lord informed of the siege.

Most of the food for the castle comes from peasants outside. They are allowed to farm the land belonging to the lord in return for some of their produce. A garden within the castle walls provides fruit trees and herb beds. Beehives are also kept for the honey.

I just caught a glimpse of my father! He's made his way through the courtyard to the battlements at the far end. Perhaps he'll be able to stop some of the archers shooting at our men below. Quick! Let's try to catch up with him. But which way?

The fighting is fierce in here. We must keep out of the way of enemy soldiers. They are desperately trying to defend their castle and will swing their swords at anything that moves! I hope father is keeping his head down.

The castle walls are built to be very thick and strong. They are made up of two walls of hewn stone blocks called "ashlar." The space in between them is filled with flint and rubble mixed with mortar. Huge chains can also be added for extra strength to help withstand the pounding from our trebuchets.

Built into the walls are compartments with narrow window slots called "loops," or "loopholes." Behind these, the castle bowmen can stand and shoot their arrows down onto us in relative safety. Even so, some of our finest marksmen can shoot an arrow through a loop from ground level and hit a bowman inside.

Towers are built on each corner of the castle and at intervals along the walls. This is to strengthen the walls and also give the defending army a position from which they can fire at us from the side if we try to scale the outer walls. Many castles have a second wall, within the first, which the defenders can withdraw to if the outer one is broken through.

A large castle can take up to 10 years to build and needs special royal permission. Many people are involved—architects, stonemasons, carpenters, blacksmiths, and laborers. Toolmakers and engineers are also employed to design and build the hoists for lifting heavy stones and timbers up to where they are needed.

Our men seem to be giving the enemy a run for their money, but we still have to gain control of the battlements and take the keep. Now we must find our way to the top of the walls where we can perhaps catch up with my father.

We have reached my father at last! But the fighting here at the keep is fiercer than ever, and we are outnumbered by the enemy. Father is worried that there may not be enough of us to take the keep and gain our victory.

The keep is the strongest and most heavily defended part of the whole castle. As our soldiers advance, the defending army retreats to the keep to protect the lord and his family. The strong high walls with towers on each corner, teeming with enemy soldiers, make it very difficult to penetrate.

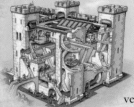

The main hall of the keep is used for most of the activities in the castle. The lord conducts all his business from there and also hosts banquets and formal occasions. Just off the main hall are other rooms, such as the "solar," where the lord keeps his bed. He and his family can retire there for privacy.

The lord's treasure is also kept safely in the keep. He has fine jewelry and expensive tapestries, but his most prized possessions are his armor and sword. The most valuable piece of furniture belonging to the lord is his bed.

Another room close to the main hall is the chapel, and there are many valuable things there, too. The Bible used is handwritten and is decorated with jewels and gold. The chapel is one of the few rooms in the castle to have glass windows. Chapels are usually placed high up in the castle to be closer to heaven.

There are many enemy soldiers here, and this part of the battle will be tough going. Father is still fighting bravely, but I think we need more men to help us before we can take the keep. I hope we can hold on until they arrive.

Start

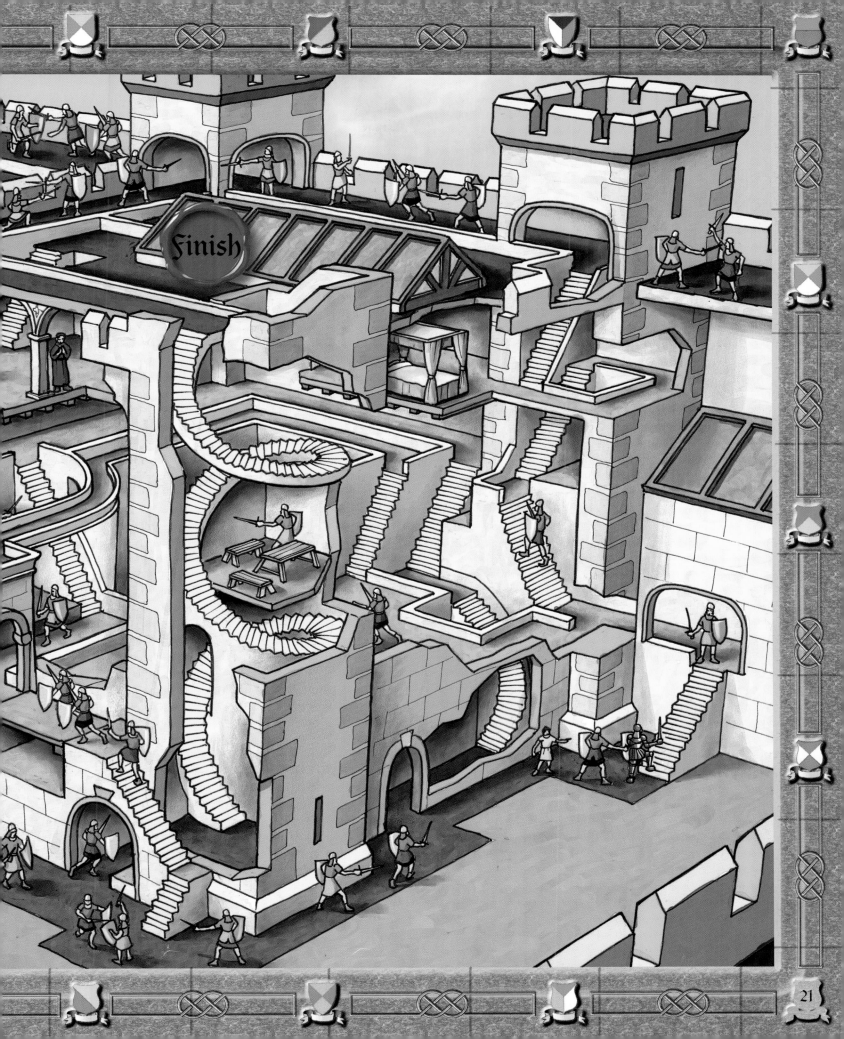

Start

Oh, no! There are too many enemy soldiers. Even my father can't beat them all. We are overpowered, and now we are to be prisoners and thrown in the castle dungeons. The siege will go on, though. Our army will not give up now. They will fight until justice is done.

The dungeons are a horrible place, deep below the main gatehouse. Sometimes, important people are taken prisoner and held for ransom. These prisoners are usually kept above ground and treated much better. Some are even allowed to roam the castle, provided they give their word that they won't try to escape.

It looks like we are heading for the dark, deep dungeons. I'm scared—the cruel lord is well known for his liking of torture. People who displease him are branded with red-hot irons, ducked in the castle moat until they almost drown, or locked in a pillory and left for people to throw things at them. Sometimes a victim is put in an "oubliette"—a small, hidden cell where he can be left and forgotten.

Most of the people judged to have committed serious crimes against the lord never get out of here alive. They are hanged at the gallows, have their heads chopped off, or are pressed to death by having weights placed on a board lying on top of them.

After torture, but still alive, some poor victims are cut open and their insides pulled out before they die. Their heads are often mounted on stakes and placed above the castle entrance as a warning.

We must find a way to escape before we are tortured. This door leads to an escape tunnel, but we must find the key. Turn the page and help us crack the code to find out where it is hidden.

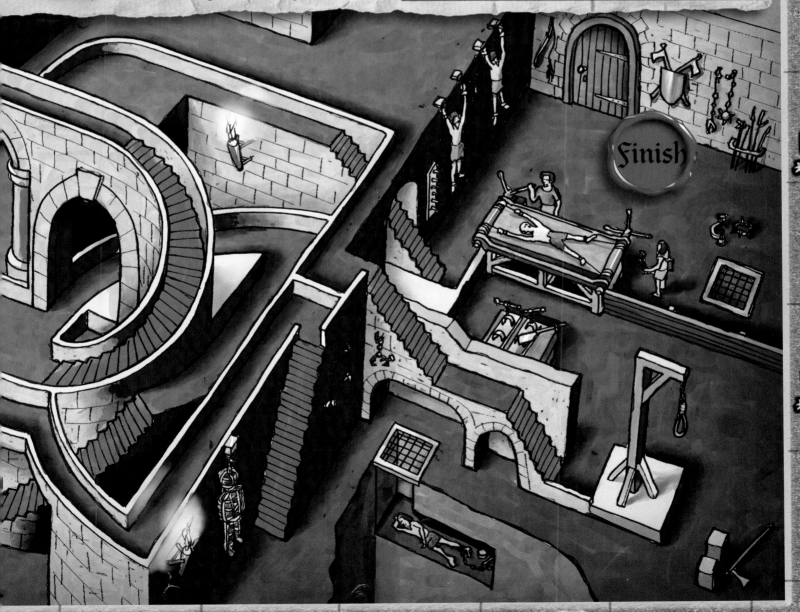

Cracking the Code

Here is a parchment prepared by the scribes of the castle. It tells the whereabouts of a hidden key that unlocks the door to a secret underground tunnel. This is an escape passage and will lead us out of these horrible dungeons to the outside world—and freedom.

But first we must crack the code that the crafty scribes have set for us and fill in the correct letters in the blank panels on the parchment. Some letters are already there. To find the others we must discover which letters each shield represents by looking at the code on the left side of the parchment. When we have all the letters written in, a sentence (without spaces between the words) should appear.

Unfortunately, though, some of the shields are blank. To find these, you must go back through the pages of this book where they are hidden. Look carefully, and you will see that each missing shield has a small symbol on its scroll. Simply find these scrolls in the borders surrounding the mazes, and there you will find the shields you need, still intact!

Remember, we can't turn the page to Maze 9 and make our escape until you have found where the key is hidden.

Good luck!

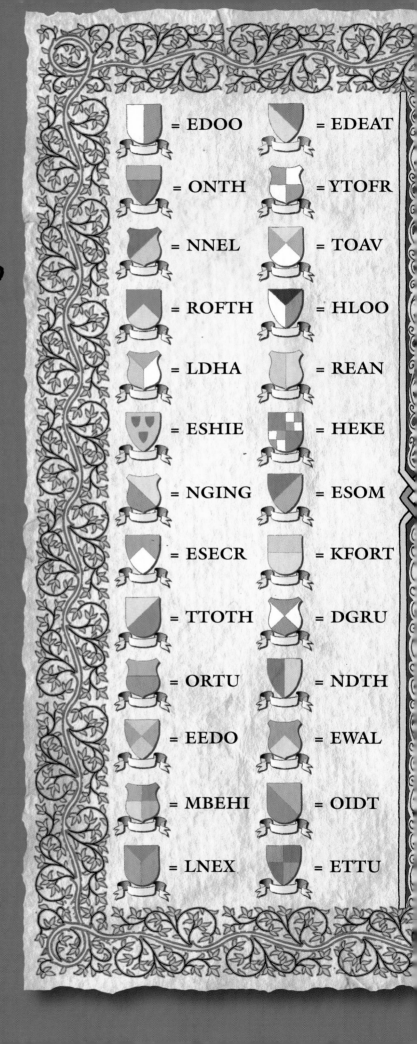

= EDOO   = EDEAT

= ONTH   = YTOFR

= NNEL   = TOAV

= ROFTH   = HLOO

= LDHA   = REAN

= ESHIE   = HEKE

= NGING   = ESOM

= ESECR   = KFORT

= TTOTH   = DGRU

= ORTU   = NDTH

= EEDO   = EWAL

= MBEHI   = OIDT

= LNEX   = ETTU

ab holte prœege et for cia guê tu ciâlti pêcœ mœtis fiuciwe. Proteg
mœtis fiuciwe. Proteg acia. Mermento inutiscloola tibi dûe quinâ
cloola tibi dûe quinâ anctœ qued noltis au tusu es cim.

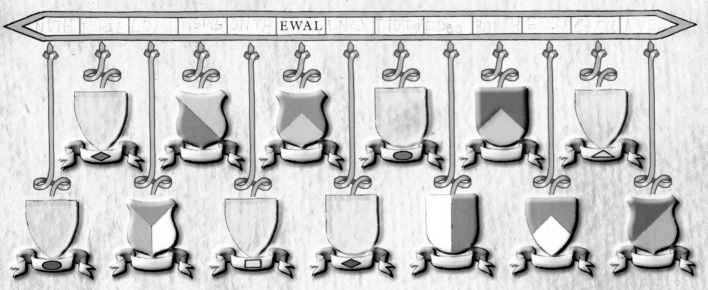

ita nnple fupena gia anctœ qued noltis au fœmam fumpleus.
cia guê tu ciâlti pêcœ rna quandi cœpus er Maria mrgiacic mater
acia. Mermento inutisillibato wigine nelœnd milfericœ die tu nos

Well done! You have helped us escape. The battle is still raging above us, but I'm sure our brave soldiers will defeat the enemy soon. We must hurry through this final tunnel before our escape is discovered.

It's a good thing that there's a secret tunnel to the outside. The castle is built so strongly that it would otherwise be as difficult to get out as it was to get in! Not only are the castle walls thick and solid, but the doors are made from thick oak panels with huge drawbars fixed across them. And metal studs in the doors blunt and break our swords and axes.

During the siege, the lord and his family have remained in the keep. This is built in a walled enclosure called the "inner bailey." Often, a gatehouse and dry ditch give it further protection.

Beyond this is a large courtyard called the "outer bailey." This is surrounded by the strong outer wall of the castle, where the large gatehouse and wide moat complete the defenses.

Even small details have not been overlooked. All the spiral staircases wind upward to the right. It is difficult for an attacking soldier climbing up the stairs to wield his sword, because the center post gets in his way.

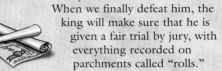

We have been lucky to make our escape. Otherwise the evil lord certainly would have had us tortured. When we finally defeat him, the king will make sure that he is given a fair trial by jury, with everything recorded on parchments called "rolls."

I can hear cheers of victory from our army—we have won! Thanks to your help, we broke so many arrows that the enemy ran out of them. An army without arrows has no chance!

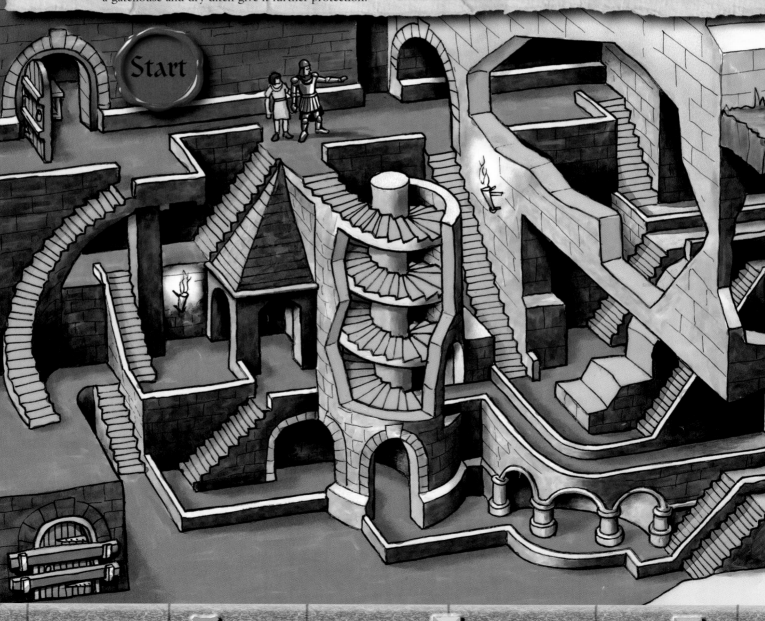

Start

Finish

Solutions

Maze 1. The Plan

Maze 2. Approaching the Castle

Maze 3. The Siege Begins

Maze 4. Breaching the Gatehouse

Maze 5. Into the Castle Courtyard

Maze 6. Seize the Battlements!

Maze 7. The Heart of the Castle

Maze 8. Captured!

To avoid torture and gruesome death look for the key to freedom behind the shield hanging on the wall next to the door of the secret tunnel.

The code cracked (use a mirror!)

Maze 9. Escape!

Glossary

ashlar
A type of smooth stone used as facing to strengthen a wall.

bailey
A court or courtyard of a castle. The walled enclosure surrounding the keep was called the "inner bailey." The large court outside this was called the "outer bailey."

barbican
An outer fortification protecting the gatehouse leading to the main entrance to the castle.

battlement
A wall or parapet with openings for soldiers to shoot arrows through or attack invaders in other ways.

belfry
A movable wooden tower used to get attackers over the castle walls.

crossbow
A bow held horizontally by the archer, who drew the string back to a hook and released the arrow by pulling a trigger. The crossbow was easier to learn to use than the longbow.

daub
A mixture of mud and horsehair used as a kind of cement in medieval times.

drawbars
Thick wooden planks secured across the inside of doors to prevent the enemy from breaking them down.

dungeons
A place under the castle where prisoners were kept and sometimes tortured.

hoist
A device used in building to lift heavy materials such as stone blocks.

keep
The stronghold, or strongest part of the castle, known in medieval times as a "great tower" or "donjon." Most medieval lords would have lived in a large stone building in the courtyard rather than in the keep.

longbow
A bow held vertically by the archer, who drew the string back and released it by hand to shoot arrows.

loops or loopholes
Narrow window slots in the castle towers through which bowmen could shoot their arrows at the invading enemy.

mangonel
A large catapult used for throwing missiles.

moat
A deep trench surrounding a castle, usually filled with water.

murder holes
Holes in the floor through which archers could shoot arrows at attackers trapped between gates on the floor below. They were also used for pouring water through to douse any fires below.

oubliette
A hidden cell under the dungeons, usually with the only opening at the top, where a prisoner could be left and more or less forgotten. It took its name from the French word "oublier," meaning "to forget."

parapet
A low wall built around the edges of a fortification to protect soldiers from enemy fire.

parchment
Animal skin used for writing on and keeping important records.

rolls
Parchments on which the records of trials were kept. They were also used for keeping accounts.

sally port
A small door in the castle wall that soldiers used for sneaking out without being seen, sometimes for launching surprise attacks.

siege
The surrounding of a fortress or town to force its surrender by attack and by cutting off supplies to the people within.

solar
A private room in the castle in which the lord kept his bed and where his family could sleep.

tortoise
The wheeled shelter that crept toward the castle and protected men filling in the moat; also called a "cat."

trebuchet
A machine used for hurling missiles at or over the castle walls from a distance.

wattle
A material used in the building of walls and roofs of medieval houses. It was made by interweaving rods and branches and plastering them together with a mixture called daub.

Index

A
animal skins 8
animals 17
archer 15
archery 17
architects 18
armor 20
armorer 17
arrows 6, 8, 15, 17, 18, 26
ashlar 18, 31
ax 26

B
bailey 26, 31
bakehouse 17
banquets 20
barbican 8, 31
battlement 17, 18, 31
bed 20
beehives 17
belfry 12, 15, 31
Bible 20
blacksmiths 17, 18
bowmen 6, 8, 12, 18
branding irons 23
brewhouse 17
building a castle 18

C
camp 12
carpenters 17, 18
cat 12
catapult 12
cattle 12
chapel 20
church 11
code 24
courtyard 15, 17, 26
crossbow 17, 31

D
daub 11, 31
defenses 8, 11, 15, 26
drawbar 26, 31
dungeons 23, 31

E
engineers 18
escape tunnel 23, 24, 26

F
fires 8
firewood 12, 17
food 17

G
gallows 23
garden 17
gatehouse 8, 15, 23, 26
geese 17

H
hall 20
hoist 18, 31
honey 17
horses 12
horseshoes 17

I
inner bailey 26

J
jewelry 20

K
keep 8, 20, 31
king 6, 26
knight 6, 8, 15

L
ladder 15
longbow 17, 31
loop 18, 31
loophole 18, 31

M
mangonel 12, 31
Middle Ages 6
miners 12, 15
moat 8, 12, 15, 26, 31
murder hole 15, 31

O
oak panels 26
oubliette 23, 31
outer bailey 26

P
parapet 31
parchment 24, 26, 31
peasants 17

pigeons 17
pigs 17
pillory 23
prisoners 23

Q
quicklime 15

R
ransom 23
rolls 26, 31
roofs 8, 11

S
sally port 15, 31
sheep 17
shield 15
siege 6, 11, 12, 23, 31
solar 20, 31
stabling 17
staircases 26
stonemasons 17, 18
storage 17
supplies 8
sword 20, 26

T
tapestries 20
tar 12, 15
toolmakers 18
tools 17
tortoise 12, 31
torture 23
towers 18, 20
treasure 20
trebuchet 12, 18, 31
trial 26
tunnel 12, 23

V
village 11

W
walls 18, 20
wattle 11, 31
weapons 17
well 11
whitewash 11
windows 20
witch 11
workshops 17